IF YOU NE

HEALING

DO THESE THINGS

by ORAL ROBERTS

FOURTH REVISED EDITION (1969)

Printed in the United States of America

A personal word

As a rebellious teen-ager I ran away from home and did not return until I was carried there and laid on my bed to die. Day after day I hovered between life and death, knowing that tuberculosis was destroying me. I felt alone. I felt utterly lost and that life was passing me by. I said bitter things to my parents. I hated my sickness. I hated the day I came into the world.

Every person who has been seriously ill and bedfast for months or years knows this feeling. A rage burns deep within at the forces which have reduced him to this condition.

Many laymen and ministers came to my bedside to pray for me. My parents constantly prayed and sought God for me. But I was not reached until somebody spoke just seven little words to me, "Oral, God is going to heal you." This is why I was saved and healed. Someone gave me hope. Someone told me that God was on my side, that He *wanted* to make me well again. God *did* heal me! And He commanded me to take this message of deliverance to my generation.

During the past two decades our vision has been to minister to the peoples of the world with the goal of seeing them made whole in mind, body and soul. God has told us to go to these millions out beyond the church walls, outside the kingdom of God. They will not come to us, but we go to them daily through the many phases of our worldwide deliverance ministry.

Because my ministry has always included praying for the physically ill, most people think that when I use the word "healing" I refer only to the healing of physical sickness. But Jesus looked upon healing as touching the whole man. He taught that when the spirit is out of harmony with God or out of harmony with people, it affects the body. Jesus saw people in disharmony with themselves, with their society, and with God; and He touched them at the point of their need.

In this book, you will learn that healing is more than physical. Healing is wholeness. And you will learn the steps to your healing and wholeness. You will learn the rules of faith for your healing and wholeness.

If You Need Healing, Do These Things, was the first book to come out of this ministry. More than a million copies have been sold. This is the fourth revised edition and it is still one of our most effectual pieces of literature in helping people to healing and wholeness.

I believe, because of my experiences, I can speak to you through this book and as you read and apply its message to your own needs, you can be made every whit whole.

Oral Roberts

Contents

Six steps to your being healed and made whole

JESUS CHRIST did not come with a life-shortening suggestion but with a life-saving power. His highest wish is for us to prosper and have health in both soul and body. He said, *Beloved, I wish above all things that thou mayest prosper and be in health, even as thy soul prospereth* (3 John 2).

The story of Jesus is the story of deliverance. In the power of His pure and healthy being and in the strength of an undivided personality, the Master of men came into this world to bring release to man from his fears and frustrations, from his spiritual, physical and mental illnesses, and to make him a whole man.

The healing that Jesus brings is more than spiritual, more than mental, more than physical—it is those and more. His healing is to make us "whole"—healthy in soul, mind and body, healthy in our relationships with others, in our attitudes, our habits, in our way of life, all the days of our life.

Jesus is a complete Deliverer from the hurts and ills of life.

A legend of the Cross

There is an old legend handed down that tells how even the wooden cross on which Jesus died brought healing:

"Helena, the mother of Constantine, while on a pilgrimage to Jerusalem, gave instructions to search for the cross of Christ. As the workmen looked through the rubbish heaps of Calvary, they found three crosses, but the inscription which was over the head of Christ was lying in a separate place. There was no clue as to which of the three crosses was the one on which our Lord died.

"Maarius, the minister of the Christian church in Jerusalem, said, 'We will test the true cross.' The sick were gathered together. They tried one cross, but there was no leaping of the lame nor opening of the eyes of the blind. They took the second cross, yet there was no response. But when they took the third cross, blind eyes were opened, deaf ears were unstopped, the lame leaped to their feet and the sick were made whole."

The wooden cross that stood on Calvary is gone. The Christ who hung thereon is ascended and reigns from heaven. Outwardly we see the cross no more. But Jesus the Person lives on, and in Him the lost, straying, suffering multitudes of every generation may find perfect deliverance. Jesus Christ is as real today as when the multitudes saw Him with their physical eyes. He is spiritual reality—the center of the plan of redemption of humanity —spirit, soul and body.

God's abundance of life

The Bible reveals a loving and helpful Redeemer. He overshadows, surrounds and undergirds those who place their trust in Him. With ever-active concern He watches over us. The details of our human existence are so important to Him that He has numbered the hairs of our head. (Luke 12:6,7.) The sparrow cannot fall to the earth without this same concern being aroused; and by Him the lilies of the field are clothed.

My life, your life, are as necessary to God's design as

the thread the weaver weaves into the pattern of his carpet. Not only am I responsible to God but also He is responsible for me. The course of our lives is His business.

God seeks to give men life—more abundant life—life in its abounding fullness of joy and strength. He is life itself and He seeks to share it with us. When the people, struggling with fear, frustration, sickness and sorrow, could get to Him, they found Him full of healing and ready to set them free. He would say, *Thy faith hath made thee whole; go in peace* (Mark 5:34). And it didn't make any difference who the people were. If they would change their attitudes and have faith, they could experience His power to make them whole.

He wanted the person to have faith in God and to change his way of life so he could use his faith to successfully meet the enemies of life.

The Bible tells of a woman, whose name was not even important enough to be recorded, who had dragged herself in and out of the hospitals of her day only to be told nothing could be done to cure her "bloody issue." One day she heard of Jesus and said, "If I can touch the border of His garment I shall be made whole." By this act she was able to release her faith. Jesus asked, "*Who* touched Me?" When the disciples reminded Him that the entire crowd was brushing up against Him, He said, "Yes, but this was a different touch." The reason was that Christ declared He felt *healing* had gone out of Him and had entered her and she was made whole.

This woman, unknown to Jesus' group, had come with her need. When she touched Him in faith, she tapped the healing power of Christ, and was instantly cured of her malady. This is a beautiful example of God's abundance of life which is available to all of us.

If this sounds too good to be true, then please read and believe this Scripture where Jesus said, *I am come that they might have life, and that they might have it more abundantly* (John 10:10). Jesus is a fountain of life and whoever turns away from sin so that his soul is unfettered and his faith can be released can receive this abundant life.

Jesus' greatest thrill is over the faith that is released for liberation from sin and from the evil powers of sickness and disease and from fear and frustration. (Matthew 8:13; 15:28; Luke 8:48; 10:17-24.) When we allow our faith to take hold of the promises of God, then God's mighty power of life surges into action in our behalf and we are liberated. God is glorified in our faith which brings His answer to our prayers.

Now, with this background, I urge you to take the following steps for your healing:

1. Know that it is God's will to heal you and make you a whole person

Practically everyone recognizes the fact of God's healing power. Mental acceptance is not enough. We must have personal, active faith in God for our own healing.

If God has ever healed one person, He will heal two; if He heals two, He will heal four; if four, then eight; and if eight, He will heal all who will believe. Else you would make Him have healing compassion for one and not another. Should that be true, He would not be God, but a man. I love God because He first loved me. (1 John 4:19.) I love Him because He loves me *and* my family *and* my friends *and* all others. I am saying this because He healed me of tuberculosis and gave me wonderful health in my entire being which I am enjoying now through His love. But should He love only me, I would be disappointed, for then if one of my children or friends took tuberculosis, it is likely (on that basis) that He would refuse to heal him.

No, you will not be able to say it is God's will to heal one but it is not His will to heal another. He is either a God of love—perfect love—or He is not God at all.

It is my sincere belief that Christ's death on the Cross was for all people everywhere and in all generations. The Apostle Peter writes of Jesus, *Who his own self bare our sins in his own body on the tree, that we, being dead to sins, should live unto righteousness: by whose stripes ye were healed* (1 Peter 2:24). More than 700 years before the Crucifixion, the Prophet Isaiah had known that Christ would be the Savior and Healer. He wrote, *But he was wounded for our transgressions, he was bruised for our iniquities: the chastisement of our peace was upon him; and with his stripes we are healed* (Isaiah 53:5).

The Apostle Matthew tells the story of Jesus as the Great Physician and at the end of the day's labor of deliverance he says that Jesus' healing power is a fulfillment of Scripture. Matthew writes, *They brought unto him many that were possessed with devils: and he cast out the spirits with his word, and healed all that were sick: that it might be fulfilled which was spoken by Esaias the prophet, saying, Himself took our infirmities, and bare our sicknesses* (Matthew 8:16,17 is referring to Isaiah 53:4).

When Jesus healed the people of their sicknesses—spiritual, mental and physical—He was freeing them from the oppression of the devil. This is made clear by Peter who said, *God anointed Jesus of Nazareth with the Holy Ghost and with power: who went about doing good, and healing all that were oppressed of the devil; for God was with him* (Acts 10:38).

Sickness is not numbered among the blessings of the gospel but is counted an enemy of human life. Jesus Christ healed the people, taking from them the heavy, oppressive hand of disease, giving them life and strength. He explained that *The Son of man is not come to destroy men's lives, but to save them* (Luke 9:56). To those of us who have received healing, this Scripture inspires us to share all we know with others who need healing.

God looks upon sickness as the oppression of the devil (Acts 10:38), as the captivity of Satan (Job 42:10), as a part of the curse of the law (Deuteronomy 28:15, 20, 22-29, 58-61, 65, 66 and Galatians 3:13), as something He himself took and bore on the Cross (Matthew 8:17), as something to be healed and destroyed by faith and prayer and special gifts (Mark 16:17,18; James 5:15 and 1 Corinthians 12:6-11).

Every act, every movement, every work of the Master was directed toward making men whole and free. When the centurion rushed up to Jesus and implored His mercy for the healing of his suffering and dying servant, Jesus replied, *I will come and heal him* (Matthew 8:7). And He did! When the little woman touched the hem of His garment by faith, healing went out of Jesus and made her whole. When the ruler cried that his little daughter was at the point of death, but if Jesus would only come and lay His hands upon her, she would not die but live, Jesus went with him and raised the child (who by this time had died) back to life. When blind Bartimaeus shouted, *Jesus, thou son of David, have mercy on me!* Jesus stopped the crowds, had the beggar brought to Him and restored his sight, saying, *Go thy way; thy faith hath made thee whole.* (Mark 10:46-52.) This is the portrait of the Great Physician. He was either on His way to heal, He was there delivering the captive or He had just left and the captive was up and rejoicing in the abundant life he had received.

2. Remember that healing begins in the inner man

You reach God and He reaches you through your soul. When God breathed the breath of life into man, he became a living soul. Jesus declares, *God is a Spirit: and they that worship him must worship him in spirit and in truth* (John 4:24).

Your soul governs your physical life and passes off to the body and mind its illnesses, its distresses and torments. As the strings of an instrument respond to the touch of human fingers, your body responds to the impressions of your soul.

There are organic and functional diseases. A person can suffer and die prematurely with either or both. The functionally induced diseases, I am told, include heart trouble, high blood pressure, mucous colitis, ulcers and certain forms of asthma. Heart disease is the number one killer of our times.

Tension, nervousness, insecurity, lack of faith, fear (both real and imagined) and frustrations are symptoms of man's soul-sickness.

Why is a man dominated by fear? Because he is not using his faith. Why is he not using faith? Because he is out of tune and harmony with his God. There is only one thing that can separate a man from God: *Your iniquities have separated between you and your God, and your sins have hid his face from you, that he will not hear* (Isaiah 59:2).

Man's most severe struggle is within himself for he is condemned by his own sins. As long as this is true, faith will not work. *If our heart condemn us not, then have we confidence* [*faith*] *toward God* (1 John 3:21).

The question presents itself, "Does a person have faith, whether he is right with God or not?"

The answer is, "Yes, he does."

Everybody has faith, for God gives a measure of faith to every man. (Romans 12:3.) The difference is that faith will not work fully, so long as sin dominates the person's life. Sin is a dominating thing and it produces a division in the soul; therefore, faith lies dormant and inactive. Without the power of active faith, the soul is no match for the grueling grind of life. The body and mind, keenly responsive to the soul, feel the impact of the soul's fears and weaknesses and fall prey to many ills.

It adds up to this: You must get right with God so God can put things right in you. Only God can heal both your inner man and outer man.

Except a man be born again, he cannot see the kingdom of God (John 3:3).

The new birth is a transforming spiritual experience. (2 Corinthians 5:17.) Condemnation is lifted. *There is therefore now no condemnation to them which are in Christ Jesus, who walk not after the flesh, but after the Spirit* (Romans 8:1).

When a person is born again by the Spirit of God, it means a change of attitudes, a change of habits and a change in daily living. *Walking not after the flesh* refers to the unselfish living of the person *in Christ*. Your attitude is important. There cannot be physical healing that will last unless a permanent change has happened in your soul. God miraculously heals the soul first. When we refuse Him that, we stop the flow of His healing power into our bodies. Let God into your soul, and you open your entire being to His healing power.

3. Use a point of contact for release of your faith

God is a Spirit and sometimes we are confused because He is not directly before us in a human body. We cannot see Him with the human eye, nor can we take a trip to heaven and present our case as we would go to our doctor's office.

How, then, can we reach Him?

By establishing a point of contact.

A point of contact is the means of sending your faith to God. A point of contact is something tangible, something you do, and when you do it you release your faith toward God.

Faith is the meeting ground between your limited self and your limitless God. A point of contact is given as a means of helping you to release your faith. Establishing a point of contact is like stepping on the starter of your car—you expect something to happen. The Roman centurion said, *Lord, I am not worthy that thou shouldest come under my roof: but speak the word only, and my servant shall be healed.* Speak the word!

He went on to say, *For I* [*also*] *am a man under authority, having soldiers under me: and I say to this man, Go, and he goeth; and to another, Come, and he cometh; and to my servant, Do this, and he doeth it* (Luke 7:6-8).

This Roman soldier is saying that he recognizes authority and is obedient to it. His master, Caesar, does not have to be present for his commands to be carried out, because the power and authority of the empire were vested in Caesar. This power was delegated to the emperor's soldiers; therefore, when the centurion gave an order to the soldiers under him, they obeyed without question.

"Now," he is saying to Jesus, "You have authority over my servant's affliction. You don't need to come to my house. I am not worthy for such an honor. Just say *the word* that my servant shall live, and I will believe it, returning home with assurance that he is well."

This is living faith—unquestioning, unfaltering, simple, childlike faith that believes God is honest and true and sends His power to accomplish whatsoever faith asks.

The Lord answered simply, *Go thy way; and as thou hast believed, so be it done unto thee* (Matthew 8:13). And his servant was healed in the selfsame hour! His point of contact was the spoken word of Jesus who had all power in heaven and in earth over human hurts and ills. The moment Jesus spoke, the centurion released his faith and his servant was made whole. This is the master key to healing.

The point of contact *sets the time.* The centurion's time for the healing of his servant was to be the very moment that Jesus spoke.

Remember that the woman with the issue of blood also used a point of contact which helped her set the time for healing. She said, *If I may touch but his clothes, I shall be whole.* There was no healing in Christ's clothes, but touching His clothes helped her release her faith, and her faith made her whole. That is why God gives us a point of contact.

The Book of Acts tells how handkerchiefs or aprons were sent from the body of the Apostle Paul to the sick and demon-possessed and how through these little faith-cloths healings were wrought. These cloths became points of contact and when placed upon the bodies of the sick and afflicted, the captives of sickness and other ills released their faith and were set free. Today, many lay their hands on their radios or television sets as a point of contact during the Abundant Life programs. Through this means they release their faith and through faith they are healed during the "prayer time" of the broadcast or telecast.

Jesus is not here today with His seamless robe, nor Paul with his blessed cloths, nor Peter with his shadow that brought healing, but God has not left himself without human instrumentalities to deliver this generation.

We read in the sixth chapter of Hebrews that the laying on of hands is a doctrine of the Church. Human hands cannot heal, but they can be instruments God uses for healing. And human hands can be the point of contact for your healing.

I believe that the laying on of hands is one of the highest expressions of the Christian faith. It is the man of God stepping beyond the pulpit, identifying himself with distressed and suffering people. It is having faith with them for their healing, and believing with them. That is one reason why I lay my hands upon the people when I minister to them in prayer.

I know that my hands cannot heal. Only the hands of God can do that. But my hands serve as a point of contact for releasing my faith for the healing of the people. When I touch someone with my hands in prayer, my heart and my compassion seem to be in my hands. All my faith, all my feeling, all the intensity of my belief in God are poured out in this contact so that everything seems to be expressed through the laying on of hands.

Jesus said of those who believed, *They shall lay hands on the sick, and they shall recover* (Mark 16:18).

James 5:14,15 tells us: *Is any sick among you? let him call for the elders of the church; and let them pray over him, anointing him with oil in the name of the Lord: and the prayer of faith shall save the sick. . . .*

Elders are the spiritual leaders in the church—ministers such as pastors, evangelists, teachers, and laymen as well. The anointing oil is a type of the Holy Spirit; there is no healing in the oil, but it is also a point of contact to help one release his faith.

Recently, a pastor of a church here in Tulsa with a membership of 1,200 called and wanted to bring his board of elders out to Oral Roberts University and have us share with them the healing ministry. We were happy to do so. They had never prayed for the sick in their church with the laying on of hands. They came and for two hours we shared with them what I am sharing with you. Now the pastor and the board of elders are laying hands on the sick in their church, and God is blessing them with definite results among their people.

This is marvelous. And it illustrates the tremendous impact Oral Roberts University will have upon the world when thousands of students—teachers, scientists, artists, ministers, etc., who have been trained by Spirit-filled teachers at the University—go forth under the power and anointing of the Holy Spirit. They will have gained more than an education. They will know how to help people find God and wholeness.

The moment another child of God lays hands upon you and anoints you with oil, release your faith. It is a point of contact.

This was my point of contact when I was healed in 1935 in a big tent revival in Ada, Okla., where the prayer of faith was made to God in my behalf.

As I was being brought to the meeting on a mattress

in the backseat of a car, after having been bedfast five months with tuberculosis in both lungs, I was led to use the anointing oil and laying on of hands as a point of contact. Down deep in my heart I was believing in God for deliverance and I told the Lord that when the evangelist anointed me and laid his hands on my head, THEN, and then alone, would I believe the work was done.

At that time I had never heard of using a point of contact for the release of faith to God. I had been taught that God used the laying on of hands in prayer for the healing of the sick, but no one had told me to make that my point of contact and at the moment hands were laid on me to send my faith to God. But this is exactly what I did and I can testify to its reality and effectiveness.

The prayer line was long. Midnight came and I was still waiting. I was suffering but I did not become discouraged or angry at having to be the last one prayed for. Trembling with anticipation, I waited for the evangelist to anoint me and touch me with his hands. At last my time came.

I was helped to my feet. I watched every move the evangelist made. Above all, I was watching for his hands to be laid on my head. Then the anointing oil touched my forehead. His hands were upon me and at that instant I sent my faith to God. The deepest desires and emotions of my hungry spirit pushed outward toward God. I believed God! I found myself thanking Him for deliverance. Every ache and pain disappeared. Glory rushed into my soul. I was tingling from head to toe with new life. And then for several minutes I was lost in the sheer ecstasy of divine deliverance. I opened my eyes a little later, astonished to realize that I was leaping and shouting and running on the long platform. I was healed! Faith had wrought it!

Oh, suffering friend, release your faith. Hang it on some Bible means of deliverance and let go of it. Hold nothing back. Pour all your pent-up faith-emotions into the act of believing God to make you whole.

4. Release your faith—now!

So many times I have seen the need of telling someone, "Believe *now* and you will have deliverance." On the other hand, many captives, if asked when they expect to get healed, will reply, "When God is ready, I am." God has been ready all the time. It is your move next. Others reply, "I'm expecting God to heal me any time." On the face of it that statement has a certain amount of value, but I remind you that it is not fully scriptural. There is a definite time when faith works and unless you set a time, it is doubtful that you will ever be delivered. God says, *Today is the day of salvation* [*deliverance*].

When you expect healing at no certain time, you are putting it into the dim, vague and distant future. God wants to heal you. The best time is when God is ready. He is ready now!

The woman with the issue of blood set a time—when she touched His garment. The centurion set a time for deliverance—when Jesus spoke the word. The ruler of the synagogue set a time—*Come and lay hands on my child*. All these expected deliverance at the moment the Lord did what they asked Him to do. God will respond and work in our behalf when we believe and set the time. This is a glorious privilege and matchless opportunity. *This very hour,* is what the Lord is saying. The longer you wait to believe, the weaker your faith will grow. The more quickly you believe, the stronger your faith will develop. Believe God for deliverance this very minute. If faith has risen in your heart, release it. Don't even finish reading this chapter. Believe God now! The time for deliverance is when you can believe. Remember, the secret of deliverance is instant obedience.

5. Close the case for victory

When Bible conditions have been met and you feel the power of healing surge through your body in answer to the faith-prayer, then close the case. Look up toward God and believe Him every step of the way. Burn every bridge between you and the old affliction. Don't talk about the affliction except when God especially impresses you to give your testimony; then dwell more on His mighty power of deliverance than on what the devil afflicted you with and how you suffered. Change your outlook and live on the sunny side of life.

6. Join yourself to companions of faith

I know how important it is to have encouragement and an atmosphere of faith to live in after having been healed.

A few days after I had been healed, I was feeling extremely weak in my body. My mother, a devout woman of faith, sensed my discouragement and said, "Son, you were sick a long time and you were bedfast for more than five months when God healed you. You will have to exercise and do some work to get your strength back. The Lord knows all about it, Son; you just keep your faith in Him." She saved my healing.

Often I have wondered what would have happened to me had not my mother and father provided an atmosphere of faith during those early days of my healing.

I have asked myself these questions: What if I had associated with a group that was unfriendly toward healing and those who had been healed? What would I have done in a moment of weakness and despondency if people had failed to encourage me or if they had ridiculed me? How could I, having been healed by a miracle, have received help from a group that denied the possibility and reality of the miracle of healing which had been wrought in me by faith in God? How would I have survived had I listened to people who ridiculed those who had prayed for me?

There is only one answer to this problem. Those receiving deliverance by faith in God should, by all means, associate with Christians who practice positive faith in God and create an atmosphere of God's love in which to live.

Summary

1. Look on Jesus as a Life-saver, delighting to bless and heal you.
2. Believe that God's abundance of life is for you and that you may have it by believing and continuing to believe.
3. Know that it is God's will to heal not only others but you also. Healing is in the atonement; therefore, it includes all.
4. Remember that healing begins within. You reach God and He reaches you through your inner man.
5. Know that the only way you can overcome fear is through your faith in God.
6. Use a point of contact for the release of your faith.
7. Close the case for victory.
8. Join yourself to companions of faith.

A dialogue with Christ for your healing

Matthew 15:22-28

HOW WOULD YOU FEEL if you discovered that your child was possessed with demons? What would you do first? Would you pray? Would you seek a higher power to deliver your child?

A woman in the Bible was faced with this problem. When there was absolutely no hope for her little girl to be restored to normal living, she did the one thing that every one of us can do. She approached God with her problem and secured deliverance, but not before she was turned down three times! And every refusal was an answer. God's *no* is just as much an answer as His *yes*. She finally understood God's answers and why He had turned her down. Then she faced herself and saw that her attitudes were wrong; her approach was wrong. She saw that she could not remake God but that He could remake her. She could not get Him to agree to her way, which would bring failure, but she could accept His way and secure the very thing she wanted most.

The fourth time she asked Him to heal her child, He responded and told her that *whatever she willed Him to do, He would do it*.

Imagine you take a trip to heaven today and bring your case before God in person: When you arrive at the gate, you meet the Apostle Peter and ask, "Peter, do you suppose He will receive me and heal my child?"

Peter replies, "Now don't you worry. He will receive

you. I have never known of His turning anyone away. You go right on in and tell Him your need."

The next one you meet is Paul. You say, "Oh, Paul, I am so glad to see you. I am going in to see God. Do you think He will grant my petition?"

Paul answers, "I was the chief of sinners and He heard my prayer, the least of the apostles and He gave me an answer. I am sure He will not turn you away."

Later you talk with John and he assures you that you will be given every consideration by the Lord.

Then they let you in and you find yourself standing before the Savior.

You say, "Oh, Master, my little child is possessed with demon spirits and I have come to You, for You alone can help me. Heal her, Lord, please."

Not a word does He answer.

You turn and stumble out. "Oh, John, He didn't answer me a word. Why, oh, why?"

"Now, don't be upset. Go right back in and repeat your request," says John.

The second time you stand there, the Master replies, "I cannot help people like you."

Once more you leave, this time badly broken. You meet Paul again. "Oh, Great Apostle, you told me He helped you and would not turn me away. But He has just said that my kind is not acceptable to Him."

Paul answers, "Didn't you wait for Him to explain what He meant by that? You didn't leave before He finished, did you? You did, I can see that. You see, Woman, God may have a better way than yours if you will only give Him a chance to show you."

The third time you stand before the Savior and plead your cause, He says, "It is not proper to give the children's bread to dogs." This is the last straw. You can take no more. Out you go. Running up to Peter, you burst into tears and say, "He called me a dog. Said I wasn't worthy. I'll never try again."

Then Peter takes hold of you and says very gently, "Woman, all that Jesus said to you was an answer."

"Why, He insulted me!"

"No, God doesn't insult anyone."

"Well, why did He say such hard things to me?"

"Whatever He said to you, He had a reason for saying it."

"You mean He did not mean to humiliate me?"

"I can assure you that what He said was intended to reveal your attitude, to help you see that the changing of your inner self often comes before a miracle of healing."

"But I want my child healed."

"I know, but the Master wants not only to heal your child but also to do something in you."

"Do you suppose . . . ? Why, I suppose you are right, Peter. The first time I came before Him, He showed no sign of recognition. Maybe that was because I wasn't in harmony with Him and wasn't seeking to be. The next time, He said He couldn't help people like me. I felt I was as good as anybody else, now I see I showed a very bad attitude. And now He says that I am a dog. Now I remember that's a word used by you children of Israel for Gentiles who do not care about God. Peter! Peter! I see it all now. He wasn't refusing me, but only trying to get me into the right condition to answer my prayer. I am going back, and this time I will know how to pray!"

This time before the Lord she said, "Truth, Lord. All you say about me is true. I am selfish and my life is not in harmony with Your life. But, Master, even the dogs eat of the crumbs that fall from their master's table. Give me a crumb, Lord."

He smiles, reaches out His hands, saying, *O woman, great is thy faith: be it unto thee even as thou wilt.* This is coming to see Christ for what He is, and seeing yourself for what you are, and seeking to change your attitude and way of life. It is also exercising your will AND your faith toward God.

There are thousands of people who are being turned down when they pray to God, all because they refuse to let God truly change them. They want God on their own terms or not at all. Consequently, they have reached a dead end; they are stymied and frustrated. Confusion torments them and they have turned away from God, ceasing even to pray anymore.

Friend, I want to share with you a way out of your dilemma, a royal roadway to the place where you can meet Christ and learn His way and follow it in life.

Here is what to do when in your prayer to God you are shown

Divine disinterest

Suppose you pray and apparently there is no word, no response whatever from God. You can't feel any assurance, any hope that your prayer has been heard. There is no tangible evidence of the answer. This means that God does not answer prayer indiscriminately.

God has given us an example of this: He told the story of a widow who was unjustly treated. The judge listened impatiently to her story and said, "Come back later."

On her next visit he was even less courteous and brushed her off. When she thought it over, she decided that her chances of getting fairness were pretty slim; that is, unless she could arouse this unjust judge. Planning her course, she went again and stood before him.

She said, "Judge, I insist on your taking immediate action!"

"Woman," he replied, "there has been a delay in your case. I am very sorry."

Once again she said, "Judge, I am not leaving until you take action in my behalf."

The judge summoned his secretary but the woman would not relent.

"I am staying right here until you help me," she said.

He looked at her and saw that she meant it and—this is important—because he saw he could not put her off any longer, he said, "Oh, all right, if it will stop you from annoying me, I will do what you say."

God says that the unjust judge avenged the woman of her adversaries, not because he was in sympathy with her cause, but because she aroused him to action by her unrelenting demands. *And shall not God avenge his own elect, which cry day and night unto him, though he bear long with them? I tell you that he will avenge them speedily* (Luke 18:7,8).

If the unjust judge would help a woman only because of her insistence, how much more will God, who is in sympathy with our cause, help those who come to Him with determination and faith.

In other words, if when you pray to God you have any thought of giving up before the answer comes, your prayer will doubtless go unanswered.

This indicates the kind of people whose prayers God answers. If you have a quitter's spirit, God will let you quit. The kind of person you are counts more than the words or petitions in your prayer.

The prayer is only as strong as the attitude back of it.

Therefore, if there seems to be no answer to your

prayers, God is seeking to change and improve the kind of person you are by causing you to reexamine yourself, to see if you have right attitudes and desires and if you have willpower and fortitude.

What to do when God says no

When Jesus told this woman that He was not sent but to the lost sheep of the house of Israel, He was saying *no* to her prayer, but not necessarily *no* to her. Before it was over, even though He had said *no,* He gave her what she wanted—healing for her child.

When God answers no, He has a better way. He doesn't mean *no* in the same sense that people do. God's refusal is subject to change when we make ourselves conform to His will and to what is ultimately best for us.

It does not mean that we are completely cut off but that we have opportunity to examine ourselves and discover if we really want healing on God's terms or only our own.

This leads me to *the thorn that God uses* and *the sickness that glorifies God.*

The Apostle Paul tells us of his *thorn in the flesh.* (2 Corinthians 12:7.) He says that it was given to him for two reasons: He had been caught up to the third heaven where he had abundant revelations. For this reason, his being a man, he was in danger of becoming proud and the people might give him more praise than he was worthy of. Hence, he says, *There was given to me a thorn in the flesh, the messenger of Satan to buffet me, lest I should be exalted above measure.*

Notice he describes his thorn in the flesh as *the messenger of Satan to buffet me.* So, then, his thorn was an evil power that brought continuous physical buffetings.

He says that this thing was so powerful that he *besought the Lord thrice, that it might depart from me. And he said unto me, My grace is sufficient for thee: for my strength is made perfect in weakness. Most gladly therefore will I rather glory in my infirmities* [*weaknesses, marginal rendering*], *that the power of Christ may rest upon me. Therefore I take pleasure in infirmities, in reproaches, in necessities, in persecutions, in distresses* [*straits*] *for Christ's sake: for when I am weak, then am I strong* (2 Corinthians 12:8-10).

Paul prayed three times. God answered each time by saying *no,* which meant He had a better and happier way. He reminded Paul: *My strength is made perfect in weakness.*

How was this weakness induced? By the messenger of Satan who buffeted or smote him with weaknesses, persecutions, straits, shipwrecks, betrayal of friendships and a long list of other opposing powers. No matter where Paul went, this messenger of evil was present to stir up the people against him. He fought with wild beasts in Ephesus, was shipwrecked three times, was beaten five times, frequently was imprisoned and was continually in danger. (2 Corinthians 11:23-30.) He said, *I die daily.*

Out of this onslaught of Satan he became weak and weary. He would pray for the thorn to be removed. God would answer, *My grace is sufficient for thee: for my strength is made perfect in weakness.* In this state of physical weakness, mental weariness and spiritual conflict Paul would cast himself utterly upon God; thus the Lord's greater strength would come upon Paul and he would rise undaunted and unconquerable. He said, *In labours more abundant,* and *In nothing am I behind the very chiefest apostle, though I be nothing,* and adds,

Truly the signs of an apostle were wrought among you in all patience, in signs, and wonders, and mighty deeds.

Through the enabling power and grace of God, Paul was able to outtravel, outpreach, outlabor, outwrite and outperform any other of his colaborers.

God had a better way for Paul. The thorn became an instrument to keep him humble and dependent on God. Paul finally accepted the thorn as God's instrument. God does His mightiest works through such dedicated people.

The sickness that glorifies God is the one He feels it best not to heal at the moment in order that it may give way to a greater miracle and serve a larger purpose.

This is found in the story of Lazarus, brother to Mary and Martha. (John 11:1-45.)

When Lazarus fell sick, his sister sent for Jesus. The messenger said to Him, *Lord, behold, he whom thou lovest is sick.* When Jesus heard that, He said, *This sickness is not unto death, but for the glory of God, that the Son of God might be glorified thereby.*

So He said *no.* Yet it is recorded that Jesus loved Martha, and her sister, and Lazarus.

In spite of this, He abode two days where He was and did not return until Lazarus had been dead and buried four days.

He had said that Lazarus' sickness was to glorify God. Jesus intended to raise Lazarus from the dead! Raising him from the dead would glorify God more than healing him. So when Jesus said *no,* He had a better way.

After Lazarus had been called forth from the grave, it is said, *Then many of the Jews which came to Mary, and had seen the things which Jesus did, believed on him* (John 11:45). Also speaking of Lazarus being alive again, the Bible states, *Because that by reason of him many of the Jews went away, and believed on Jesus* (John 12:11).

Don't be afraid to trust God for He knows what He is doing and knows best how to bless and to guide you.

What it means when God says wait

When God says *wait,* it means that in a special way His will or purpose is involved. In other words, it is more important to wait a little while for the working out of certain details in your life, for certain changes to be wrought, than it is to answer you instantly. This is very true in healing. In some cases, God heals instantly but where a higher purpose is involved, He says *wait.* When His will has been worked out, then the healing can be received.

When Jesus told Mary and Martha to wait, His will was to perform a greater miracle so that many more would believe on Him. Thus He was able to accomplish more by the delay.

However, there may be an enforced wait that God has not caused.

When Daniel prayed unto God for His blessing, the devil hindered and the man of God had to wait 21 complete days for the answer. It was not because God would not respond, or that He said *no* or *wait,* but demons were directly opposing (Daniel 10:11-13.)

It happened in this manner:

The devil has authority as the *prince of the power of the air* and has headquarters between this earth and heaven where God's throne is. Daniel prayed in Babylon and the prayer was received in heaven. God dispatched the answer through regular channels. The demon hordes of Satan kept the answer bottled up for 20 days. Daniel continued to believe, refusing to give up. Although he could not understand the seeming delay, he would not quit praying. On the 21st day, God told the mighty angel Michael to take the answer through the enemy lines to His beloved servant.

Michael stormed the devil's fort, pushed through the demon guards, lifted the gates off Satan's inner sanctum, reached in and got the answer to Daniel's prayer and kept right on going. When Michael arrived in Babylon, Daniel was on his face before God. Michael raised him up and said, *O Daniel, a man greatly beloved . . . from the first day . . . thy words were heard. . . . But the prince of the kingdom of Persia* [*refers to demons*] *withstood me one and twenty days.*

If you pray in all sincerity and faithfulness according to the will of God and the answer will not come through, you may know that the devil has thrown up a blockade. Hold on; God will get the answer through even if He has to put His mighty angels on the case. They will get the answer through to you, if you have held on.

Finally, Jesus told the woman, *It is not meet to take the children's bread, and cast it to dogs.*

Remember, she came to ask Christ to heal her little demon-possessed child and Jesus replied that she was asking for the *children's bread* which He would not give to her because she was *unclean* or not right with God.

Healing *is* the children's bread. This is why He is so careful to lead her on, to probe her soul, to work a change in her life, to get her into the attitude of humility, love and faith.

Jesus indicates that healing is the heritage of His children. Thank God, it is. This is one of the most amazing revelations Jesus ever made. *I am the Lord that heal-*

eth thee (Exodus 15:26); *Who forgiveth all thine iniquities; who healeth all thy diseases* (Psalm 103:3).

Each one of us has a perfect right to God and, just as He will forgive all our sins, He will heal all our diseases.

Then this woman showed the spirit of humility. When she saw the truth of Christ's statements, she admitted she was not in harmony with God. She saw that her way of life was wrong, yet she was asking for healing.

She humbled her spirit and acknowledged that she needed His saving power, saying, "Truth, Lord, I am unclean and not in the least worthy to sit with Thy children." She felt sincerely the sense of unworthiness which motivates true healing.

Then she said, *Yet the dogs eat of the crumbs which fall from their master's table*. In other words, "A crumb, please." She asked for only a healing crumb because she felt unworthy to sit with the children. "Pitch it under the table, Lord," she was saying with modesty, determination and humble devotion.

Jesus was thrilled and immediately cried, *O woman, great is thy faith: be it unto thee even as thou wilt.*

O Woman. . . . By her willingness to change her attitude and enter the kingdom of God, she caused Christ to think of her as *an individual*. Her faith put Him to work in her behalf. Faith is always rewarded. The key to things we need is our faith in God.

A little girl is tormented with a demon. Her mother now is standing before Jesus in sincere worship and faith. Jesus, removed by a great distance from the child back in her home, responds to the mother's faith by saying what He will say to any of us who will humble ourselves and believe Him, *Be it unto thee even as thou wilt.*

She can now have her need met. It was. *And her daughter was made whole from that very hour.*

Nothing is too hard with God. He can do all things and do them well. He wants to give us more than a physical healing; He wants to make us what we ought to be; He wants us to bring our whole person into harmony with Him.

There is no doubt about it, you get results when you pray. When your prayer is backed up by the right attitude, when you are willing to change your way of life, when you approach Christ with firmness and determination—you will be heard, you will be received.

Summary

1. If there is no answer to your prayer, there is a reason.
2. Your attitude is more important than the words of your prayer.
3. If there is no indication that your prayer has been answered, it may be that God is seeking to work a change in you.
4. When God says *no,* it indicates He has a better way.
5. His delay in answering your prayer means His will for your life is involved or the devil is opposing in a special manner. In either case, don't give up—keep asking God.
6. Remember, healing is the children's bread. You have no right to healing until you change and bring your life into harmony with His. Once you have changed your ways and received Christ, it is your heritage. Have faith and you can be healed.
7. Faith is always rewarded. Through your will exercised firmly toward God you can release your faith. God will answer you.

Seven rules of faith you can use today for your healing

2 Kings 5: 1-15

OUR STORY centers around a famous man, General Naaman of Syria. Naaman was commander-in-chief of Syria's expeditionary forces, and, because of his outstanding military successes, had been hailed as a national hero.

It was shocking news when the general's personal physician found his chief had contracted leprosy which was widely prevalent in those days.

Across the nation, the cry went up, "General Naaman is a leper! Our beloved leader is a leper!"

Leprosy meant living death—slow, torturous, isolated suffering.

Disease is a foul and inhuman thing and is not numbered among the blessings of life. Jesus Christ came against it in the power of His pure and healthy humanity, laying His healing hands upon the sick and tormented, *healing every sickness and every disease among the people* (Matthew 9:35). People touched Him, too. The Bible record states that *as many as touched him were made whole* (Mark 6:56).

In the story of Naaman's miraculous healing through his faith in God, there are seven rules of faith that we can use today for healing.

Rule one: Recognize sickness and disease as the oppression of the devil

This rule of faith is made plain to us by the leading member of the Twelve Apostles—Simon Peter. The great Apostle knew the Savior's love for suffering humanity. After the resurrection of Christ, the Apostle was preaching to the soldiers in the house of Cornelius in Caesarea. He said, *God anointed Jesus of Nazareth with the Holy Ghost and with power: who went about doing good, and healing all that were oppressed of the devil; for God was with him* (Acts 10:38).

Healing all that were oppressed of the devil; this is Peter's summation of the ministry of the Lord Jesus.

Satan, Peter is saying, is a destroyer of human life, while Jesus is a destroyer of the oppressions (human afflictions) of the devil.

The writers of the Four Gospels—Matthew, Mark, Luke and John—tell the story of Jesus and His healing power. All of them tell how Jesus found the people oppressed with all manner of sickness and all manner of disease and demons. They tell how He healed their sick. (Matthew 4:23; 14:14.)

They tell how compassion flowed through Him like the water of a pure mountain stream and became healing virtue for all who would believe. (Mark 5:30.) The healing virtue of Jesus is God's antidote against disease and is available now to all who will send their faith to Him.

The Savior did not turn any person away who had faith. Making no differentiation as to race, He looked for faith and wherever He found it He healed the sick. One of His favorite expressions was, *As thou hast believed, so be it done unto thee* (Matthew 8:13).

He healed the blind, the deaf, the crippled, the demon-possessed, the feverish, the brokenhearted and many others.

Those so afflicted were classified by the Apostle Peter as being oppressed. He saw these oppressed people healed by the Master.

Later, Peter in writing the first of his New Testament books declares, *by whose stripes ye were healed* (1 Peter 2:24).

Healing power was given to the followers of Jesus Christ and many of them were outstandingly successful in delivering the people. (Matthew 10:1.) Peter's shadow was used as a *point of contact* and those upon whom it fell were healed. (Acts 5:15.) This was after the Day of Pentecost. Similarly, Stephen and Philip, laymen of the Early Church, through faith, brought outstanding healings to many oppressed people. (Acts 6:8; 8:5-8.)

Paul describes the nine gifts of the Spirit in 1 Corinthians 12, including the gifts of healing, the gift of faith, the gift of discerning of spirits, and the gift of miracles. These gifts are mighty in healing the sick and casting out demons. They are additional stimulants to faith and will bring deliverance when other means fail.

Any gift from God is to be used for the deliverance of others—not for personal gratification.

This, then, is our God: loving, tender, compassionate and full of healing power. It is wise to know the difference between Satan the oppressor, and Christ the Lifesaver. (John 10:10.) Just as Satan is the source of all human torment, God is the source of life. Christ's healthy, undivided personality is for men and women everywhere who want health, peace and happiness.

Remember, the Bible pictures Jesus as coming into a

world full of sickness and demon oppression. When the religious leaders of Israel would not work with Him, He went alone; yet not alone, *for God was with Him* (Acts 10:38). He chose men and women to be His partners and through them He transmitted His healing power.

He had glorious success in healing the souls, minds and bodies of the multitudes. He never said to one, "It is *not* My will to heal you," and to another, "It *is* My will to heal you," but He healed all those who were oppressed of the devil and who would believe.

Only once are we told that He was powerless to heal. But even this had a reason. The people of Nazareth were His boyhood acquaintances and they were skeptical; they looked upon the accounts of His wonders with cynical scorn and when He came to preach to them, they met Him with cold unbelief. The Gospel writers do not omit this failure of Jesus in His hometown but record it in a terse, tragic sentence: *And he did not many mighty works there because of their unbelief* (Matthew 13:58).

This means that in the use of His miraculous power, He requires faith in those who would be healed.

His deep sorrow is traceable not only to the power of Satan over mankind but also to the unbelief of the people He came to deliver.

The most thrilling question ever asked by the Son of God is, *Wilt thou be made whole?* His answer then was the same as it is now, *Rise, thy faith doth make thee whole*. Faith does it.

God, who is busy with the affairs of an entire generation, has the time and power and desire to save, to heal, to reward and bless. Wherever there is human need, He is present to heal. (Luke 5:17.)

The power of God to heal human life is still active

today—in the faith and love of His people in all churches and in all walks of life. God honors their faith for their faith honors God.

Remember, rule one of faith is that Satan is the oppressor of human life; God brings life with health, peace and happiness.

General Naaman had made a victorious march across the Bible land of Israel and had taken captive a little maid to be servant to his wife. This child was familiar with God and His prophets and knew they could heal. Seeing the general was a leper, she said, *Would God my lord were with the prophet that is in Samaria* [*Israel*]*! for he would recover him of his leprosy*.

Naaman was grateful for this hope, believed the little girl's message and made preparations to leave at once for Israel.

Rule two: Believe the message

What matter if the message came from a servant girl? The message of God is more important than its messenger. Oh, that all of us would believe this. We are becoming so denominationalized that we all but demand that God's messenger be a member of our particular denomination or church. We lose sight of the importance of the message because of our insistence that the messenger carry our own label. God does not place as much stress upon our different theological emphases as we do. In becoming narrow and bigoted in our theologies and creeds, we place ourselves in the same position as the disciples who were sternly rebuked by Christ: *And John answered him, saying, Master, we saw one casting out devils in thy name, and he followeth not us: and we forbad him, because he followeth not us. But Jesus said, Forbid him not: for there is no man which shall do a miracle in my name, that can lightly speak evil of me* (Mark 9:38,39).

This is Christ's indictment against sectarianism.

When Christ said, "You are to take My healing power to your generation," He gave me a ministry that transcends denominational barriers. Our ministry is filled with God's love for *all people*. This same dimension is in the new Oral Roberts University in Tulsa, Okla. The school is interdenominational. It operates to educate the whole man regardless of who he is or where he comes from.

It has been our experience that God does not compel us all to wear the same denominational label, but rather that we love one another and work together to win souls.

The little Jewish maid said, *Would God my lord were with the prophet that is in Samaria! for he would recover him of his leprosy*. This is also the basis for

Rule three: Go where the power is

Israel represented God; and Elisha, who lived there, was God's prophet. Syria was a land of idol worshipers, and Naaman had to get away from the old haunts of sin and get close to God. "Go where the power is," the little girl was saying, "back to God, back to moral vows and saving religion."

This is a profound truth—God is everywhere present because He is omnipresent and omnipotent. His all-prevailing power is usable by the person who maintains right attitudes and whose faith creates an atmosphere conducive to divine deliverance.

Even in His day, Christ found that some places were antagonistic to His truth. He bitterly denounced these cities. (Matthew 11:20-24.)

This may come as a shock to you. You may have to change your entire way of life—your thoughts, your attitudes, your purposes, your goals.

Why? You must get over on God's side!

General Naaman acted upon the advice of the little maid and set forth on his trip to the land of Israel. But he made a serious mistake. Instead of going to the prophet, he went to the king of Israel. The king was outraged and declared he could do nothing for him. About that time a messenger came into the king's court with word from Elisha, *Let him come now to me, and he shall know that there is a prophet in Israel.* This is important for it has to do with

Rule four: Put your faith in God, not man

The little girl had clearly told Naaman that the prophet would teach him how to use his faith to be healed of leprosy. Instead, he had gone to the king.

I cannot insist too strongly that you put your faith in God. Have *confidence* in His servant or prophet, but put your *faith* in Almighty God, not man.

The person God has chosen to help you receive healing is an instrument only—the means to an end. Your deliverance is by faith in God and His power.

Naaman rode up to the house of Elisha and sent his servant to announce his arrival. Being forewarned of God that Naaman's attitude would have to be changed and discerning the general's pride and arrogance, the prophet acted accordingly.

Elisha was the servant of God—the human instrument only. He was in the delicate position of having to deal with a proud, dying man and having to govern his acts according to the rules of faith. Faith had to be aroused in Naaman; otherwise, he would have returned home with his leprosy. To be healed, a man's heart must be right with God and his soul in tune with his Maker. *God, not the prophet or preacher, is the Healer.*

I have been faced with the same conditions many times in our crusades across the world where the multitudes have thronged for our ministry of faith and love. To show a man his condition, pointing out the rules of faith so that God will honor prayer for him, is a serious assignment for any servant of God. But that is the preacher's charge.

In order to receive healing from God, who is love, the seeker must be a partaker of that love. Faith is based on love. How else could God believe in us, or we in Him? To believe, one must love. An attitude of selfishness, pride and stubbornness makes it impossible for faith to be fully released. When God's minister is being used of God to help you, let wrong attitudes give way to love, making it possible for you to be healed by the power of God.

With great detachment, Elisha remained in his house. He sent the famous general a message by his servant: "Sir, the prophet said for you to go and dip seven times in the Jordan River and your flesh shall be clean" (paraphrased).

Naaman was astonished, then enraged and finally commanded his aides to depart at once. As he went away, he muttered, "Go dip in that filthy river? Bah! I thought the prophet would at least come to me and do some great thing and heal me. If I wanted to bathe, I would have stayed at home. At least, the water in the rivers of Syria is clean."

Elisha saw him leave and perhaps said, "Yes, that is the way it goes with the proud. They are bound by their own little concepts and notions, never once thinking that when they ask for healing they are dealing with Jehovah God and that there are rules which govern faith. Humility, respect for God's message and His prophets, a desire to give up sin and to worship the true God—these attitudes help a man get in harmony with God and help him believe."

Many precious people are letting some preconceived idea or prejudice keep them from being healed. This thought occurred to one of Naaman's servants who said, "Master, we want our lord to be recovered from his leprosy. The prophet is right, Sir, you *were* expecting the prophet to do some great thing over you and because he did the opposite you were offended and now you are returning unhealed. Master, in your servant's humble opinion, it is better to go wash and be clean."

What a wonderful way to reason things out.

Rule five: Accept the correction of God

Naaman listened and when the servant had finished, he nodded his head in agreement. "You are right," he said. "I am wrong. I did come here self-centered and proud. Ah, this Elisha is a great one—saw right through me. And his God must have shown the prophet the kind of man I was. 'Go dip in the Jordan,' the prophet says. Surely I can do that. Let's go."

It takes a humble spirit for one to change like that. This is a marvelous thing. It doesn't take long for a man to change if he wants to. But he must want to. When he accepts God's correction, the Spirit of Christ enters him and he is a "new creature"—*old things are passed away; behold, all things are become new* (2 Corinthians 5:17). Repentance is a change of mind before it becomes a change of heart.

General Naaman gave the order and they went to the river. With Elisha's message ringing in his ears, *Go and wash,* he plunged into the muddy, yellow waters of the famous River Jordan. As he did so, there were only a few ripples on the water revealing that the great man was *all under*. This is the accomplishment of

Rule six: Lose yourself

What a contrast! The man who went to the wrong place for healing, who was rude to God's prophet, who was bound by his own creeds, who was a very angry man, the man who had refused to obey, a famous but dying man, was now losing himself.

There are a lot of things we would be better off *without*. Losing ourselves in obedience to God, linking ourselves with the limitless power of Christ, getting in tune with the Savior—these are the things that count most when we seek to be healed through faith in God. Lose yourself. (Matthew 16:25.)

Naaman had come a long way since he had left Syria. Who would have believed the national hero would be dipping in a river, despised by his countrymen? But there he was and enjoying every moment of it.

Something was going on in Naaman's spirit. He was willing, joyously willing, to make the sevenfold plunge. Through it he believed he would be cured. This led to what many believe to be the most important rule of all—

Rule seven: Use a point of contact and become as you want to be

The Prophet Elisha had said that if Naaman would dip *seven times* his flesh would be cleansed from leprosy. What is this but a point of contact or a means through which he could release his faith? He was to dip seven times—no more, no fewer—in a designated river. He would find by the time he became willing to do this he would be in the right attitude, the proper frame of mind, to believe for a miraculous recovery.

He said, "Now I see it all. This is to prepare me for believing that God will heal me."

He dips once, twice, thrice . . . and the seventh. He is all under. His pride is under, his attitude, his all.

"Just this seventh time and it will be done. I know God will heal me."

Your point of contact can be one of several things. Mine is my right hand. Though there is no healing virtue in my right hand, God spoke to me and told me that I would feel His power through my right hand. It is a sensation of God's presence. When I lay my hand on the head of the person seeking God's healing and begin to pray, I often feel this power going through my right hand. The moment I feel it, my faith is very strong. This point of contact helps me release my faith to God. Also, it helps the person seeking healing. When my faith and his faith make contact with God, the healing begins. This is the point of contact we use in our crusades, either through my hands or those of our team members. However, there are many other ways—such as the anointing oil of James 5:15, the laying on of hands in Mark 16:17, and the blessed cloths of Acts 19:11,12. What does it matter what the point of contact is if it helps you release your faith?

Naaman came up out of the water the seventh time crying, "I've done it! I've obeyed! Now the Lord God will heal me."

With unhampered faith in a limitless God, he walked out on the river bank, believing his leprosy would go.

He had done what the prophet said. He had brought himself into harmony with God. He released his faith and . . . it happened!

And his flesh came again like unto the flesh of a little child, and he was clean (2 Kings 5:14).

He was so grateful that he returned to the prophet's house but, as befits all true servants of God, Elisha would accept no gift for the miracle wrought.

The general made his vows to the true God that he would worship Him and henceforth would serve no other gods.

What a fitting climax! He obeyed the rules of faith and found a new life. But he did not forget the God who had healed him. His leprosy was gone and God had come into his life.

What God did for Naaman, He will do for you.

Summary

1. Recognize that sickness is the oppression of the devil and that God wants you to be well and happy. (Acts 10:38; John 10:10.)
2. Believe the message of deliverance, no matter who is God's messenger.
3. Go where the power of God is, even though you may have to change your attitude and way of life.
4. Put your faith in God, not man. Remember, the man of God is an instrument. God is the Healer.
5. Accept God's correction for He knows best.
6. Lose yourself, for then you can become a new person.
7. Use a point of contact and be healed, a whole person again.

Touching Christ to be made whole

Mark 5:25–34; Luke 8:43–48

THIS IS THE STORY of a woman who touched the hem of Jesus' garment and in return was made a whole woman. This Bible drama will show you how to release your faith even in the most difficult conditions. Once you have released your faith it will release healing power, causing it to flow into your being where it will destroy disease and affliction.

The name of the woman who touched the hem of His garment is unknown. Her name is not recorded in the Bible. I think this is because God would have us draw courage and inspiration from her story by putting our name where hers could have been. Then we, too, will release our faith, not by putting our hands on His clothes as she did, but by using some other point of contact which will enable us to believe Christ for our deliverance and receive from Him a healing just as glorious as she received.

Seven things happened in her life which can be very real for us today.

1. She came to the end of her own way and stopped before she went to pieces

The Bible says that she had an incurable disease. She had an issue of blood for 12 years. Perhaps it was a bleeding cancer. We don't know. But there seemed to be something causing the issue of blood which could not be cured. *She had suffered many things of many physicians, and had spent all that she had, and was nothing bettered, but rather grew worse.* She had spent every penny she had to regain her health but her affliction grew steadily worse.

One day she faced her problem and realized that she had exhausted medical science, as well as her money. She saw futility, and she made a remarkable decision —to stop before she went to pieces. She knew where she stood; she was beyond human help.

She came to the end of her own way and stopped. It could be said, "She came to the end of her rope and hung on." Fear sets in when we know there is no cure; yet we frantically keep seeking human aid. But she stopped before fear could tear her to pieces.

2. She heard the story of faith—and believed it

The story of Jesus reached her. There was a Galilean Prophet who was going throughout Judea healing the sick and bringing peace to their souls. So remarkable was His power that totally blind eyes had been opened by His touch; the deaf and dumb now heard and spoke; even some of the hopeless cripples were made whole. Naturally, great crowds were thronging Him, insomuch that He hardly had time to rest or eat. The multitudes were so thick around Him that there was little opportunity to talk with Him or have Him put His hands upon one. But His ministry had inspired such faith that now the people wanted only to touch Him, and it was reported that everyone who came close enough to touch even His clothes was perfectly healed.

His name? Jesus of Nazareth.

It was astounding news but the woman believed it—every word of it. Anyone who can believe in human skill can believe in God's power. For what man can do partially, God can do completely; and what man cannot do at all, our heavenly Father can do.

The story they told her about Jesus of Nazareth is the same one I heard when I had tuberculosis. I believed it and through it I found the way to faith and hope and was healed. It is the same story I tell the masses, face-to-face in our evangelistic crusades and to those who hear the message on our radio and television programs.

I ask you to believe this story of faith, for I know that through it you can do something about your frustrations, fears, and illnesses.

This woman said to herself, "How wonderful this man must be! He heals those who just touch Him. That is the most amazing thing I have ever heard! When they can't get any closer, they can reach out and touch Him and He heals them. Think of that!

"If He can do it for them, He can do it for me. If they can touch Him, I can too. Oh, if I can touch just the hem of His robe I know He will make me whole."

With these words she set her point of contact. If she could but touch His clothes, her faith would be released. This means that

3. She created a faith-image of Jesus and of being healed by Him

When the woman heard of Jesus and believed to the extent that she could set her point of contact, then Jesus became real to her. He was no longer a name or a symbol or a hope to others. He became *a Person* to her — One who could give back her life, her health. Her mind was filled with Him. Long before she saw Him, all other persons faded from her mind. The failures of the past faded away. All other ideas faded. All her other plans were laid aside so that her one plan was to make contact with Christ.

The Bible says, *When she had heard of Jesus . . . she said, If I may touch but his clothes, I shall be whole.* She saw Him in her mind before she saw Him with her eyes. She saw herself there touching His clothes, feeling His healing virtue and being restored to health—all this before she ever went to Him.

So the woman's point of contact made her Christ-conscious. It put her mind in the right condition for healing. There was no room for fear because her mind was filled with Christ. She knew the source of her healing was a Person and when she saw Him she would believe and be made whole.

4. She touched Him for a cause

After she had touched Him and had felt that she was whole of her plague, she *declared unto him for what cause she had touched him.*

Her cause was to be made whole. For that purpose she touched Him.

Life is a whole—a unit. You are a spirit made in the image of God. You have a mind with a free will, you live in a body or house of muscle and bone. But you are a person consisting of spirit, mind and body, all working together as a whole.

This woman conceived of her whole self being made whole by touching Jesus' clothes. This was her cause, her dream, her goal. And this is why Jesus had come. He was within her reach when she came to touch Him.

5. She used a point of contact to touch Him differently

Her point of contact was touching the *border of His garment*.

There was no healing in His clothes, for He said to her, *Thy faith hath made thee whole*—not the touching of His clothes. It was her faith. But He did not rebuke her for touching His clothes because she touched them as her point of contact. She felt that by touching the robe He wore she could believe. Sometimes people find that touching a prayer cloth or putting one upon their bodies helps them release their faith. There is no healing in the prayer cloth itself, but in the faith that is released to God.

God will honor any point of contact that will help us release our faith.

As she made her way through the crowd, she was saying, "If I can only touch His clothes; if I can only touch His clothes!" Her faith cleared a path for her feet and made an opening through the crowd for her.

The people were pressing so closely together that the only way she could have got through was by faith. Faith will move God and man. It will take you through when everything else fails. Have faith in God.

The crowd moved back for her, and she pressed on through, and then . . . there He was! She had made it through to Him. She bent low, reached out a trembling hand and *touched* the hem of His garment. In a sense, it was like touching a live electrical wire. The mighty healing power of Christ surged from Him to her. It went all through her, into every fiber of her being and spent its force against her affliction. In a moment's time *she felt in her body that she was healed of that plague*. Notice, *she* was healed; not only her body, but her whole self.

Hundreds of people were around Christ. But the woman was the only one there who touched the power of God. Jesus turned around and said, "Who touched Me?"

Peter said, "Lord, what do You mean? The crowd is jostling up against You."

"Yes, but this was a different touch," Jesus indicated. "I felt healing power go out of Me."

Oh, Friend, believe it. Jesus is full of healing virtue! He is charged with the mighty power of God to make you *every whit whole!*

Hers was a different touch! She touched Him not as a part of the crowd but as an individual. She touched Him knowingly, believingly, purposefully, as a point of contact. She touched His clothes with a specific purpose—to let her faith go to God. The moment she touched His robe she believed. Right then! That is the way to use a point of contact. The virtue in Jesus heals on contact, bringing deliverance from disease and fear and frustration—and healing *you*.

She said if she could touch Jesus' clothes, then and there she would believe that He would heal her. And it happened.

It would have happened had she used some other point of contact, as long as she would have believed then and there.

This is the thing you must grasp and understand. There is more than one point of contact, for God cannot be limited to any special thing or to any certain person.

The simple use of a point of contact is to help us connect with the healing virtue of Jesus.

The Apostle Paul sent handkerchiefs from his body

(that he had prayed over) and, although there was no healing virtue in them as such, they were used as points of contact. The people knew the cloths had been prayed over by Paul and that there was power in his prayers. The moment the handkerchiefs were placed upon them —that moment, I say—they sent their faith to God and He healed them. *And God wrought special miracles by the hands of Paul: so that from his body were brought unto the sick handkerchiefs or aprons, and the diseases departed from them, and the evil spirits went out of them* (Acts 19:11,12).

The faith-cloths that we pray over are to be used as points of contact and in the same manner that God brings deliverance through faith in His name.

6. She made contact with healing power

She felt in her body that she was healed of that plague. Contact was made between her faith and the healing virtue resident in Jesus Christ. As plugging into an electrical connection makes contact with the distant powerhouse, faith that is released—put into action— makes contact with God's power and releases His healing power. This power healed the woman of disease and made her whole.

7. The faith she released made her whole

When Jesus asked, *Who touched me?* the woman saw that she could not be hidden and came trembling before Him. She told Him why she had touched Him and how she had been healed.

Jesus said, *Daughter, thy faith hath made thee whole; go in peace, and be whole of thy plague.*

The woman received even more than she had hoped for. She had felt that her need was physical healing. But

He gave her what her whole inner being had been crying for—peace.

By connecting peace with healing, Jesus is saying, "You sought healing for your body. But healing is much more than a physical work. Healing is also a spiritual work. Wholeness is healing for the soul, mind and body. Your faith has made *you* whole."

Let us remember this: Healing from God is both physical and spiritual. Suppose the woman had received physical healing alone. She would have had healing for her body but not the peace of God in her soul. But when she looked to Jesus for her complete healing, her mind became centered in Him. When she touched His clothes, she was filled with His power and made whole.

Friend, what she did, you can do. She sent her faith to God and so can you. God is a good God and He will reward your faith with deliverance.

Summary

1. When you come to the end of your own way, stop before you go to pieces.
2. Believe the story of deliverance and that it is for you.
3. Make a faith-image of Jesus—and of being healed by Him.
4. Life is a whole. Christ seeks to give you life more abundantly. Think in those terms.
5. Use a point of contact to touch God differently. Your faith will lift you out of the crowd.
6. Make contact with Christ's healing power by sending your faith to Him. He heals on contact.
7. Remember that your own faith will make you whole. God rewards those who have faith. Your faith released to God will make you a whole person again.

Raise the roof and be made whole

Luke 5:17–26

IN LUKE'S ACCOUNT of the healing of the man with palsy we have one of the most remarkable examples of wholeness in the New Testament. Two things stand out in this man's deliverance: his own terrible physical need of healing, and the presence of the Lord to heal him. God's power to heal is always present when someone is sick or afflicted.

God loves you, is near you and wants to heal you. However, there is no magic connected with divine healing. You are healed by faith, and faith alone—active faith that forges ahead in spite of every hindrance, every adversity—faith that sometimes has to "raise the roof" to get the victory. Healing does not come except as we meet Bible conditions.

Shaking with a severe case of palsy, shut in and shut out from the world of normal well people, this afflicted man was a victim of the tormenting, afflicting, enslaving power of the devil. God did not place this disease upon him nor was God receiving any glory from its terrible effect upon his life and home.

Jesus came to bring life. He came not to afflict but to heal, not to destroy but to save, not to impoverish but to enrich, not to drag down but to lift up, not to send to hell but to take to heaven. Jesus Christ came as a Healer, a Deliverer, a Lifesaver.

Satan is a destroyer and oppressor. Friend, don't blame God for your hurts and ills, for *every good gift and every perfect gift is from above, and cometh down from the Father of lights, with whom is no variableness, neither shadow of turning* (James 1:17).

Meanwhile, Jesus had returned to Capernaum. He was staying in a certain house which already was crowded with people who had heard He was there. They had come from every quarter to see and hear the mighty things of God. Even the Pharisees and doctors of the law were present. So great was the multitude that *there was no room to receive them, no, not so much as about the door* (Mark 2:1).

Luke significantly adds: *And the power of the Lord was present to heal.* Hallelujah! Wherever Jesus is, the power of the Lord is present to heal. This is God's provision for our deliverance from the oppression of the devil. Jesus was then, and is now, concerned with the needs of suffering humanity. He wants to set us free, and will, when we believe in Him and release our faith.

Jesus was always ready to heal the oppressed. Whenever the captives could go where He was, they found deliverance. They believed Him for healing of soul, spirit and body. Too long we have separated all but our soul needs from Christ's atoning work of Calvary. We have spiritualized the gospel to where it is a force for the soul, but not for the body; whereas, all the teaching of Jesus is one for the whole being of man—soul, mind and body. As the Savior delivered all who came unto Him then, so will He meet our needs today through His mighty healing power.

The power of God to heal is present today, and whenever and wherever believers will exercise faith, they may *lay hands on the sick and they shall recover* (Mark

16:18). This is not only our privilege but also our responsibility. As believers we are vested with power to heal the sick, to cast out devils and to bring deliverance, by faith, into the lives of those bound by the devil. (Matthew 10:1, James 5:15,16.)

James says, *Pray one for another that ye may be healed.* We have the responsibility to assist those suffering under the devil's oppression in a personal, brotherly manner and to bring healing to one another.

Four men in Capernaum took the palsied man into their sympathies and resolved to bring him to Jesus for deliverance. Compassion springs from divine love and is more than mere human sympathy. True compassion is identification with the person in his suffering until you feel you must do something to get him delivered.

Having compassion for a helpless neighbor, these four men took his case into their own hands, bringing him to Jesus, since by himself he could not attend the healing service in Capernaum.

Before the four men took up the corners of the mattress upon which lay the helpless paralytic, they pledged themselves to bold, direct action. They set out for their goal—deliverance at any cost.

Jesus had been in their city before and His work of compassion to all who came for deliverance had convinced them that He would turn none away.

Confident that if they got their afflicted friend where Jesus was conducting a service he would return home *every whit whole,* they began pressing their way through the blockade.

This is the goal of every intercessor. Determine in your heart and mind that Christ must be reached. Know that you will reach Him as you press your way through. *He that cometh to God must believe that he is, and that he is a rewarder of them that diligently seek him* (Hebrews 11:6).

When they arrived with their charge, the four men of compassion found the way to Jesus blocked with the press of the people. As they advanced, seeking an opening, they were pushed back. They kept trying but each time the human blockade stood in the way. Now what could they do? There was no opening in the crowd. Apparently they must return home defeated. But, no! Refusing to turn back, they

Burned their bridges

Here is the secret of deliverance. Healing is for those who forsake not their bold, determined efforts to be healed but who burn the bridges between them and the affliction.

The story is recorded that Julius Caesar, having determined to conquer Britain, sailed with his legions from France to England. Then he burned every ship used for crossing the English Channel.

It was either conquer or die! There could be no retreat!

Many more would be healed today if they would not give up when the way is temporarily blocked.

How many times the four men tried to get their friend in to Jesus we do not know, but it must have been several. One thing was fixed in their minds: they would not turn back!

When all available means of getting to Jesus failed, these men of compassion threw caution to the winds and resorted to drastic action.

They raised the roof for victory!

Here was a case of affliction beyond human cure; only

Jesus could heal him, but the human blockade was between him and deliverance. Daring to go beyond the conventional, tossing pride aside, these men turned away from the crowd with a divinely conceived plan. With boldness, they climbed upon the housetop and began tearing off the roof. Hallelujah! This is the crowd I want to be identified with—the roof-raisers! It is time to raise the roof for our needs and get in where the Lord's power is present NOW to heal.

These men were "partners for deliverance." They felt they had a job to perform—to get their suffering friend healed. There should be purpose to every Christian's life. The purpose of Jesus was to deliver humanity. We are His followers. Can we do less?

God has promised victory to partners for deliverance. *Where two or three are gathered together in my name, there am I in the midst of them,* Jesus said. (Matthew 18:20.) And remember that wherever the Lord is, His power is present to heal.

Faith that works

While Jesus was preaching to the people inside the house, there was a commotion on the housetop. These men were tearing off the tile roof.

As the debris filtered down into the house, the doctors of the law murmured their disapproval. They felt that such action was out of place since it interrupted the service. There are those today who are alarmed at the demonstration of someone's faith to reach Christ for healing. But since God specializes in the impossible and deals in the supernatural, as shown by divine creation and divine redemption, we have a perfect scriptural right to believe and make strenuous efforts to receive divine help.

Jesus was never alarmed by someone's faith for deliverance. He was there to *preach the gospel to the poor . . . to heal the brokenhearted, to preach deliverance to the captives, and recovering of sight to the blind, to set at liberty them that are bruised* (Luke 4:18).

When the opportunity to deliver came, Jesus always went into action, setting the captive free. He preached to build faith, for *faith cometh by hearing, and hearing by the word of God* (Romans 10:17). When Jesus saw faith, He stopped whatever He was doing and answered it.

Thank God, we are seeing this today.

The purpose of our gospel services is to inspire people to believe in God. We should never be so tied to convention, to human plans, to a set pattern, that we will not stop everything—anytime—to bring deliverance to the souls and bodies of those in need.

Looking up through the opening in the roof, the Master saw a couch being lowered by four pairs of strong hands. Then He saw something else, something He always looks for before He is moved into action.

Luke says, *He saw THEIR FAITH.*

Their faith was responsible for this scene. Their faith, having set as their goal deliverance at any cost, had burned every bridge and now, after tearing off the roof, presented the patient to Christ the Healer.

Faith is the victory! Thousands will never find deliverance unless we manifest faith in their behalf. Believing with others for deliverance is not only our privilege but also our responsibility.

Burning his bridges

The faith partners had done all they could. Their faith had completed its mission. The roof was raised, an opening large enough to get him through to Jesus had been made and the palsied man was where the power of the Lord was present to heal.

It was up to him now.

There is a time and place where you are on your own. When you get where the Lord's healing power is, *you* must believe. *You* must act. *You* must become a roof-raiser, too.

Jesus said to the man, *Arise, and take up thy couch, and go into thine house!*

It was time now for the palsied man to have personal faith, to set his goal and burn his bridges, to break every connection with the affliction and actually believe NOW for deliverance. Others had told him of the Master, others had brought him to the healing service, others had raised the roof for victory, others had brought him where the healing presence of Christ was—but that was not enough. There is no magic connected with healing. Jesus always told the captive to do something, then He said, *THY FAITH hath made thee whole.* The thing we must help you do is to release your faith. Get it into action. Faith accomplishes things only as it is *released*. You can have faith only as you exercise it. If you were to place a perfectly normal arm in a sling and keep it there in a state of inaction for several months, it would become useless. It would become stiff. You may have faith lying dormant in your soul, but it will bring deliverance only as you use it.

The palsied man had been bedfast for a long time. His limbs were incapable of lifting and supporting his body. He had to sever all connections with past defeats, with present afflictions and hopes of future freedom. His faith had to act. Jesus was saying, "*Arise!* Arise in the inner man first. Then take up your bed and walk." The inner man standing up inside helps the outer man take new strength into the body.

Without hesitation the palsied man recognized the authority of Jesus over his affliction; and without questioning Christ's command of faith, *Arise, and take up thy couch, and go into thine house,* he made a gallant effort to rise. And to the astonishment of the crowd, he actually *rose up before them, and took up that whereon he lay, and departed to his own house, glorifying God.*

There are no bonds that faith cannot break, no fetters it cannot sever, no dungeon it cannot open, no disease it cannot heal, no victory it cannot win. Faith puts you directly into the hands of a limitless God who *is able to do exceeding abundantly above all that we ask or think, according to the power that worketh in us.*

Suffering one, don't try to believe tomorrow or next week or sometime in the distant future—believe *now.* There was a time when this man could have the miracle of healing wrought in his entire being—that was the moment Jesus told him to arise!

The secret of deliverance is instant obedience.

You can have this, too

When the man arose under the mighty power of God as it penetrated every fiber of his body, the crowd moved back to let him through. His destination now was home, sweet home. For months he had been bound to his bed, shut in from the world and alone in his misery. The devil had stolen the bloom of health and kept him bound to the couch. But faith had set him free.

Throwing his little mattress over his shoulders, he leaped and ran through the crowd, out the door and down the highway toward home. As the people saw him go, they glorified God and said to each other, *We have seen strange things today*. They were impressed more with this one healing than they were with all the cut-and-dried church services they had ever attended. God was able to get nearer to them than at any time before. There is something about God's love and concern and healing for the captives of Satan that touches the hearts of men and draws them toward God. The Bible says, *The goodness of God leadeth thee to repentance* (Romans 2:4).

There is only one way to reach the world for Christ today and that is to bring this mighty power of deliverance by faith as partners for deliverance. We must have revivals to bring healing to the whole man. The power of God must fall upon us, the power of the Lord must be present for our deliverance. The hurts and ills of humanity must find deliverance in our prayers of faith. Dare we fail God and suffering people in this crucial hour of the world's need? Shall we sit supinely by while Satan is ever busy in his work of human oppression when the only kind of revival conducted by Jesus, the 70 apostles, the deacons and missionaries of the Early Church was to heal men in soul, mind and body? Why not now? Let us raise the roof for victory!

You cannot get healed without getting a blessing for your soul. The same Christ who healed the palsied man's afflictions also said to him, *Man, thy sins are forgiven thee*.

The man went home saved and healed. He was *whole*. Place yourself in the position of this man who found deliverance. Strike a blow for your deliverance. Do something! Raise the roof for victory! Deliverance is yours now, by faith in the same Christ who healed the palsied man and who lives today to meet your needs.